BY WATER AND THE SPIRIT

What it means to be baptised

A commentary on the services of baptism and confirmation

CHURCH OF SCOTLAND
OFFICE FOR WORSHIP AND DOCTRINE

SAINT ANDREW PRESS
EDINBURGH

First published in 2006 by
SAINT ANDREW PRESS
121 George Street, Edinburgh EH2 4YN

on behalf of the
OFFICE FOR WORSHIP AND DOCTRINE
of the CHURCH OF SCOTLAND

ISBN 10-digit: 0 86153 372 0
ISBN 13-digit: 978 0 86153 372 5

British Library Cataloguing in Publication Data
A catalogue record for this book is available from the British Library

Typesetting by Waverley Typesetters
Printed and bound by Mackay & Inglis Ltd, Glasgow

PREFACE

Baptism with water in the power of the Holy Spirit is the means of entry into Christ's Church. This booklet is designed for those who wish to explore the Church's beliefs about baptism and membership, especially those who seek baptism for themselves or their children.

It takes the form of a commentary on the services from *Common Order* 1994/1996/2005, on the basis that what Christians do and say when they worship is one of the best indicators of what they believe.

For this purpose, the orders relating to children and adults, together with the order for Confirmation/Admission to Holy Communion, have been combined into one continuous order. On each facing page, under quotations from the relevant part of the service, is a commentary which aims to draw out the meaning of what is happening. To assist the eye, the phrases quoted are printed in bold in the order of service itself.

In the course of this commentary, 'performance' suggestions are offered which have been found to heighten and enhance the impact of the event (these are distinguished by boxed text). These, however, should never be allowed to 'eclipse' the central act.

The commentary has been written in the light of the report on baptism given by the Panel on Doctrine to the General Assembly of 2003, which resulted in changes being adopted by the Church in relation to its baptismal practice and to the Act which enshrines this. As well as offering direct quotations from this, the main conclusions of the report are incorporated in the commentary.

The 2003 report itself is available separately from the Office for Worship and Doctrine: wordoc@cofscotland.org.uk, 0131-225 5722 ext. 359.

September 2005

Douglas Galbraith
Co-ordinator (1995–2005)
Office for Worship and Doctrine
Church of Scotland

Order for Holy Baptism with Admission to Holy Communion/Confirmation

Sections particular to the baptism of infants are printed against a shaded background. Please note that the left-hand pages contain a compilation of three related services and cannot be used for leading worship.

Those coming, or being brought, for baptism may be accompanied by members of their families, and by their district elders.

Normally, the Sacrament is administered during Sunday worship, usually after the sermon.

1   **Words of Institution**

The minister says:

The Gospel tells us that
'**Jesus was baptised in the Jordan by John.**
As he was coming up out of the water,
he saw the heavens break open
and the Spirit descend on him, like a dove.
And a voice came from heaven;
"You are my beloved Son;
in you I take delight".'

St Mark 1:9–11

Jesus himself said:
Full authority in heaven and on earth
has been committed to me.
Go therefore to all nations
and make them my disciples;
baptise them in the name of the Father
and the Son and the Holy Spirit,
and teach them to observe
all that I have commanded you.
I will be with you always, to the end of time.

St Matthew 28:18–20

The Gospel tells us ... Jesus himself said ...

Baptism is known as a 'sacrament'. This part of the service bears the title 'Words of Institution' because of the understanding that a sacrament, to be a sacrament, must have been 'instituted' by Christ himself – in this case, by his own action in being baptised and in his instruction to his followers to baptise, recorded in these first two Scripture passages. Holy Communion, which also flows out of an action by Christ himself and an instruction to his followers, is the other sacrament observed in most Reformed Churches.

In sacraments, we receive ordinary material things of life, like water and wine, and through them the grace of God is conveyed, as Jesus Christ has revealed it. Through word and action, there is an appeal both to the understanding and to the senses, powerful enough to incorporate us in events otherwise beyond our grasp. By an action as well as by a word, we are helped to enter into a holy mystery. 'Sacraments are like the handclasp which accompanies "Hello", like the kiss that accompanies "I love you!" In the sacraments, God touches our bodies and we see, feel, smell, taste and hear God's life-giving Word' (Harold Daniels). They do not 'make something true'; that has already happened. Through word, water, wine and bread, the Holy Spirit carries the full impact of God's greater gift. In baptism, the greater gift is Christ reaching out to take us into himself so that our lives are transformed.

When should baptisms take place?

Baptism should take place among the people who are to nurture the baptised persons in their growth in faith, most appropriately when the congregation gathers for worship. In that context, placing it after the preaching of the Word of God and in the same position as the Lord's Supper, as the rubric suggests, emphasises that what gives rise to baptism is the 'Word made flesh' reaching out graciously towards humankind. A baptism should not be seen as a substitute for a children's address, nor should a need to fall in with the arrangements for the Sunday School dictate how baptism should be handled.

66To suggest that something is 'symbolic' should not be thought of as meaning that it is 'merely symbolic'. Instead, we should think of the act of baptism as symbolising the deep and richly significant act in which God bestows the Holy Spirit. That is not to say that we should link the gift of the Spirit exclusively to the act of baptism. It is to say that the act of baptism symbolises the giving of the Spirit in a particularly significant way.99 (Report of the Panel on Doctrine, 2003)

On the Day of Pentecost, the Apostle Peter said:
Repent and be baptised, every one of you,
in the name of Jesus the Messiah;
then your sins will be forgiven
and you will receive the gift of the Holy Spirit.
The promise is to you and to your children
and to all who are far away,
to everyone whom the Lord our God may call.

Acts 2:38–9

In addition, one or more of the following may be read:

Isaiah 43:1–2a	*I call you by name; you are mine*
Ezekiel 36:25a, 26a	*I shall sprinkle pure water over you*
Luke 18:16–17	*Let the children come to me*
John 3:5–7	*You must all be born again*
Romans 6:3–4	*We were baptised unto his death*
Ephesians 4:4–6	*One Lord, one faith, one baptism*
Titus 3:4–7	*He saved us through the water of rebirth*
1 Peter 2:9	*You are a chosen race, a royal priesthood*

Jesus was baptised in the Jordan by John ...

Our baptism begins with Jesus' own baptism. All the careful detail given in the gospels suggests the importance of this moment, for Jesus himself and for all who were to follow him thereafter. This was no morning service over by lunchtime but a 'liturgy' which lasted a lifetime, culminating not when Jesus was raised, newly baptised, from the river but when he was delivered, newly alive, from the tomb. This is how he saw it himself, and why he asked his disciples: 'Are you able ... to be baptised with the baptism I am baptised with?' (Mark 10:38).

For us also, baptism is the beginning of a journey, a journey measured not in miles or years but in a deepening ability to love God and neighbour. Christ has invited us to find life for ourselves in the life he has already led in obedience to God. However, in a real sense, it is not our decision, nor, in the case of infants, their parents' decision, to become a follower of Christ. The initiative is Christ's alone. It is he who has planted our steps on the way; our life thereafter is a moving forward on that way as his disciples. That it is God who calls us, not we who decide to 'take up God' or religion, was also the teaching of the apostle Peter at Pentecost. The third of the readings, from Acts 2, is a reminder, too, that baptism is an event of joy, excitement and celebration rather than simply a 'rite of passage'. It will always be a matter of wonder that we should be chosen in this way.

> **"**Baptism, in terms of its signifying the action and love of God in Christ, through the Holy Spirit, is the gift of God that most clearly calls the people of God to their unity in Christ.**"**
> (Report of the Panel on Doctrine, 2003)

The time for baptism

Early in the life of the Church, baptisms took place during the Vigil leading to Easter morning, or at Pentecost. Today, in addition to these, other suitable times could be the First Sunday after Epiphany (when the baptism of Christ is remembered), or All Saints' Day, or the day on which the saint who gives his/her name to a local church is commemorated, or on a congregational anniversary.

---

2 **Statement**

The minister says:

When Jesus was baptised
in the waters of the Jordan,
the Spirit of God came upon him.
His baptism was completed
through his dying and rising again.

Our baptism is the sign of **dying to sin
and rising** to new life in Christ.

It is Christ himself who baptises us.
By the Spirit of Pentecost,
he makes us members of his body, the Church,
and calls us to share his ministry in the world.

By water and the Holy Spirit,
God claims us as his own,
washes us from sin,
and sets us free from the power of death.

In this sacrament,
the love of God is offered to each one of us.
Though we cannot understand or explain it,
we are called to accept that love
with the openness and trust of a child.
In baptism,
N ... is assured
of the love that God has for *her*,
and the sign and seal of the Holy Spirit
is placed upon *her*.

Dying to sin and rising ...

This is the first of three striking pictures used in the New Testament to show the meaning of baptism. The apostle Paul speaks of being buried with Christ 'by baptism into his death' so that we might walk in newness of life (Romans 6:3–4). God in Christ entered our human weakness, suffering and death. In his baptism-life, Jesus challenged and overcame evil in its most destructive form. In his death and resurrection, he re-established the bonds between person and person, between creation and Creator, between the physical and the spiritual. In being baptised, we acknowledge all that Christ has done and receive his healing power into our lives.

That is not to deny that we still may have to confront problems, to encounter setbacks and to brave dead ends – but evil no longer has the casting vote. Our transformation is not simply spiritual. We are also freed from fear in our actions and attitudes towards other people and are enabled to contribute to transformation in the life of our communities, where 'there is no longer Jew or Greek ... slave or free ... male and female' but all are 'one in Christ Jesus' (Galatians 3:28).

He makes us members ...

The second picture is of new birth. We later pray (p. 14) that we might be 'born anew of water and the Holy Spirit'. Whether it be soon after our natural birth, or many years later, we are delivered by baptism into a new humanity, shaped by the life and continuing presence of Christ. We are born into a new and wider family, that of the Church, the 'household of faith', where we can find the right kind of nourishment to grow in the direction of Christ.

God ... washes us from sin ...

The third great picture is that of washing. The fresh start of forgiveness that we receive on each Lord's day has its prototype in our baptism. Later in the service, adults seeking baptism are asked: 'Do you reject sin and confess your need of God's forgiving grace?' (p. 10). After his dramatic conversion, Saul, the former persecutor, is invited by Ananias to be baptised and have his sins washed away (Acts 22:16). In baptism, once and for all, our tendency towards sin is turned round (early Christians physically turned from facing west to facing east) so that all our actions are now tested against God's love rather than measured against our failings.

Procession to the font

Depending on the font's position, some congregations process to it as a body with the family, signifying that this baptism is given not to one person but is a gift to the whole Church, and to indicate their intention to continue to participate in the growing life of the person being baptised.

Either

3 **Confession**

The minister says to the parents/godparents/sponsors:

In presenting this child for baptism,
desiring that *she* may be grafted into Christ
as a member of his body, the Church,
do you receive the teaching of the Christian faith
which we confess in the Apostles' Creed?

I do.

or

3 **Profession of Faith**

The minister says:

In seeking baptism,
do you reject sin
and confess your need of God's forgiving grace;
and, believing the Christian faith,
do you pledge yourself to glorify God
and to love your neighbour?

Each candidate answers:

I do.

Confession ... Profession

'Confession' or 'Profession' – this seems to suggest a parting of the ways. In 'profession', the baptised person answers for him/herself, while in 'confession' parents or godparents/sponsors are asked about their faith. However, baptism is baptism regardless of age or level of maturity. At whatever age we come to baptism, we are to accept the love God offers 'with the openness and trust of a child' (the Statement at 2, p. 8). If baptism is a journey of growing 'into Christ', it is one which can begin at any age, even early in our growth as human beings. Learning about life, learning how to trust and to love, the developing of gifts and talents: that is for all ages.

A very young child cannot choose to be baptised, nor can s/he respond in faith; but this only highlights the fact that baptism does not take place as a result of our decision but is an action of God who reaches out to us irrespective of the level of our understanding. Just as a parent in caring for a young child does not withhold love until it can be returned, so God shows his love to those who may not be able to respond. In the New Testament, when someone was baptised, it is recorded that other members of the household were baptised also (Lydia, Cornelius, Crispus, the Philippian gaoler – Acts 16:14–15, 11:13–18, 18:8, 16:31). While it is true that the New Testament's primary image is of persons being baptised on profession of faith, it is complemented by this model of the baptism of households, seen as a collective whole rather than as a collection of individuals.

Infant and adult baptism thus emphasise different parts of the same truth. Baptism, whether of an adult or a young child, proclaims and conveys the grace of God. In the case of an infant, we see vividly that God moves towards us in love in spite of the fact that we have done nothing to 'deserve' it. With an adult, we are reminded that the Christian life is one lived in a responding faith. It is the same baptism, and that is why the service is virtually the same for adults as for children.

There is an important connection between Christian baptism and the biblical theme of *covenant*. The Covenant in which God made gracious promises to Abraham and Sarah and their descendants had circumcision as its sign. For Paul, the new covenantal relationship promised in Jesus Christ grew out of and derived part of its powerful meaning from this 'old covenant' (Galatians 3:6–18), baptism being the sign parallel to circumcision, with the difference that, whereas circumcision signified male entry into a particular nation, the 'New Israel' of baptism is potentially open to all comers and both sexes. The early Church also saw the passing through the Red Sea as an 'old covenant' baptism (1 Corinthians 10:2), with its climax in the Covenant made at Mount Sinai (Exodus 24:7), and allowed this powerful story to bring out the dimension of deliverance to freedom which is given to those baptised into Christ.

The minister says:

Will the congregation please stand.

Let us affirm the faith.

I believe in God, the Father almighty,
creator of heaven and earth.

I believe in Jesus Christ,
God's only Son, our Lord,
who was conceived by the Holy Spirit,
born of the Virgin Mary,
suffered under Pontius Pilate,
was crucified, died, and was buried;
he descended to the dead.
On the third day he rose again;
he ascended into heaven,
he is seated
at the right hand of the Father,
and he will come to judge
the living and the dead.

I believe in the Holy Spirit,
the holy catholic Church,
the communion of saints,
the forgiveness of sins,
the resurrection of the body,
and the life everlasting.   Amen.

The minister says:

Let us pray.

I believe ...

This affirmation of faith is known as the *Apostles' Creed*. It is a statement of faith which is believed to have started life in the vows made at baptismal services early in the Church's history and had taken this form by c. AD 750. That is why some Churches at this point in the service insert instead the three separate questions and answers from which the Creed may have developed: 'Do you believe in God? ... in Jesus Christ? ... in the Holy Spirit?' – 'I believe ...'.

In the Creed, as well as making our own response in faith, we are also affirming the faith of the whole Church. It is not, at base, because of our faith that we present ourselves for baptism but because we have been called to a life of faith; we are baptised *into* faith. Faith is not 'believing certain unbelievable things' intellectually but putting our lives in other (God's) hands, trusting God to turn us round towards ways that enrich life and express God's love – in terms of new knowledge and insight, of our feelings and emotions, of our ethical behaviour. The journey of which we have already spoken is one made *from* as well as *to* faith.

Through the Church's experience, beliefs and practices, we learn faith and its meaning. In speaking of the 'Church' here, we mean not only the local parish church, or a particular denomination, but also the whole Church together, called in the Creed 'the holy catholic Church' (*catholic* means 'universal' and includes the Church world-wide and stretching back in time). Most main branches of the Church recognise the 'validity' of each other's baptism. In fact, baptised persons may receive a certificate not solely from their own Church but 'signed' by several denominations in the UK.

The holy catholic Church

To emphasise the fact that baptism in one congregation is baptism into the whole Church, some congregations invite one or two representatives from neighbouring congregations of other denominations to be present at, and perhaps participate significantly in, services where baptism is to take place.

---

66 The early Christians instinctively turned to their experience of baptism to throw light on various issues they faced in their Churches ... One thing that was fundamentally true of them and bound them together was that they had all been baptised into Christ. 99 (Report of the Panel on Doctrine, 2003)

4   **Prayer**

We thank you, gracious God,
for your gifts of water and the Holy Spirit.
[In the beginning, you moved over the waters
and brought light and life to a formless waste.
By the waters of the flood,
you cleansed the world,
and made with Noah and his family
a new beginning for all people.
In the time of Moses, you led your people
out of slavery through the waters of the sea,
making covenant with them in a new land.
At the appointed time,
in the waters of the Jordan
when Jesus was baptised by John,
you sent your Spirit upon him.
And now, by the baptism
of his death and resurrection,
Christ sets us free from sin and death
and opens the way to eternal life.]

The minister may pour water into the font.

Send your Holy Spirit
upon us and upon this water,
that *N* ... ,
being buried with Christ in baptism,
may rise with him to newness of life;
and being born anew of water and the Holy Spirit
may remain for ever
in the number of your faithful children;
through Jesus Christ our Lord,
to whom with you and the Holy Spirit
be all honour and glory, now and for ever.
                              Amen.

Send your Holy Spirit upon us and upon this water ...

Jesus clearly accepted water as a significant element in his baptism; and, for a 'life and death' event such as is baptism, **water** is most eloquent and suitable. Water is there at the beginning of life as we are kept in the waters of the womb. It sustains and enhances life as it refreshes, cools, cleans, offers beauty (in rivers, falls, breakers, snowflakes). But the power of water is also capable of ending life when it overwhelms and destroys.

This thanksgiving prayer recognises the part water has played not just in human life but also in God's dealings with humankind. An element of creation, water has been an eloquent symbol of how God led his people to freedom, parting the waters to ease their flight during the Exodus from slavery in ancient Egypt. For Noah, the terrible judgement of the floodwaters also symbolised a new beginning in a cleansed world. In the waters of baptism, freedom is not just from physical slavery but also from the crippling and destructive effects of sin and death.

But water is just water, however rich in imagery and meaning, until the **Holy Spirit** acts upon both the water being used and the people present in the event of baptism. Thus we pray: *Send your Holy Spirit upon us and upon this water.* God claims us as his own not just by water but also by the Holy Spirit. Together they are the 'sign' and 'seal' of our baptism. A sign translates into the language of the senses a real event which cannot be experienced directly; and a seal secures it fast.

The Spirit not only is active in the rite of baptism but also works towards the spiritual regeneration of the baptised person. In the gospel of John, being 'born of water' is linked to being 'born of ... the Spirit' (John 3:5). This is not to suggest a 'mechanical' connection between the act of baptism and the arrival of the Holy Spirit. This great gift to humankind is God's to bestow and to bestow freely. Rather we should say that the act of baptism marks the giving of the Spirit in a particularly significant way. In baptism, this life flowing through the Church catches up individuals and sweeps them into the Church and along Christ's way.

> **66** Baptism signifies the action and love of God in Christ, through the Holy Spirit, and is a seal upon the gift of grace and the response of faith. **99** (Report of the Panel on Doctrine, 2003)

5 **Declaration**

For each child/candidate, the minister says such words as:

N ...,
for you Jesus Christ came into the world:
for you he lived and showed God's love;
for you he suffered the darkness of Calvary
and cried at the last, 'It is accomplished';
for you he triumphed over death
and rose in newness of life;
for you he ascended to reign at God's right hand.
All this he did for you, *N ...,*
though you do not know it yet.
And so the word of Scripture is fulfilled:
'We love because God loved us first.'

6 **Baptism**

The minister pours or sprinkles *water on each*
child's/candidate's head, saying:

N ..., I baptise you
in (*or* into) the name of the Father,
and of the Son,
and of the Holy Spirit. **Amen.**

For you Jesus Christ came into the world ...

This moving declaration, first used by the French Reformed Church, brings home the truth that God's great act of salvation through Christ which shook the world and brought hope to humanity was directed just as much at individuals. The one to be baptised is here addressed directly.

The minister pours or sprinkles water ...

To carry meaning, the water used should be plentiful, enough for people in (usually) a largeish building to see it properly and be convinced that it is really there. The water may be poured into the font in the sight of the congregation, possibly by the appropriate district elder, so that as well as being seen its splashings are heard. At the act of baptism, the water should be sprinkled liberally or poured three times on the child's or adult's head (some use a shell as container) so that it is seen by all and felt by the one being baptised. Some churches have baths into which the candidate for baptism goes down, is immersed, and re-emerges, symbolising dying to evil and rising to new life. There is nothing in our understanding of baptism to rule out any of these uses; the only thing that is discouraged is to use so insignificant an amount of water that the meaning is obscured.

In the name ...

The momentous words which go with the vivid action of pouring water are much more than mere formula. Whenever they are said, the Church glimpses the movement that is within God, the interplay between the Father, Son and Holy Spirit who reaches out to embrace the new Christian and the whole world. Here is a God who moves within and between people and communities, creating and re-creating. In baptism, we are caught up in the exuberance of God, in what someone has called the 'dance of the Trinity'.

❝Our baptism is performed 'in the name of the Father and of the Son and of the Holy Spirit'. This form of words has come to be regarded by the Church Catholic as having universal significance and its use is shared across the whole Church. Therefore, the Church of Scotland recognises and affirms the validity of an act of baptism administered in the name of the Father and of the Son and of the Holy Spirit, with water, in every branch or member of the Catholic or Universal Church ... Baptism links us into the world Church, and gives us a place within, and a concern for, the rich tapestry that is the history of the universal Church.❞ (Report of the Panel on Doctrine, 2003)

15

7   **Blessing**

The minister says:

The blessing of God Almighty,
Father, Son, and Holy Spirit,
descend upon you,
and dwell in your heart for ever.   **Amen.**

*This blessing may be **said or sung**:*

The Lord bless you and keep you;
the Lord make his face to shine upon you,
and be gracious unto you;
the Lord lift up his countenance upon you,
and give you peace.   **Amen.**

The minister says:

N ... is now baptised into Jesus Christ.
We receive and welcome *her* as a member
of the one holy catholic and apostolic Church.

We receive and welcome ... as a member ...

Baptism signifies and marks Christ finding us and accepting us, but this is not a purely private matter between God and an individual. It is the Church, the body of Christ, which at Christ's bidding 'Go therefore and make disciples' finds and welcomes the individual into its midst. In the shared faith of the Church we discover our own faith; in the community in which all are together as one in Christ we discover what love means; in the body whose head is the Christ who is to come again and renew all things we discover the hope that we must share with all people – confronting despair, loneliness and injustice with the message of the Good News of Jesus Christ.

The baptised person belongs now in a new community, joined to Christ and to the Church, which is called 'Christ's body'. An individual may try to follow the Way of Jesus, but it takes all the 'members' of the body of Christ together to experience fully at first hand all that Christ wrought and all that God did in him. In the Church we learn obedience, love, expectancy, goodness, freedom. Through others we recognise and are given the courage to develop our own special gifts and graces. We are kept in union with Christ by the reality of our being together in the Church, a fellowship which is understood to embrace those who have gone before us in time and those still to come.

The fact that baptism is now one of the chief talking points among the Churches of the world, and the best hope of greater unity, underlines the need for the Church to reclaim baptism and restore it to its rightful place, not least its importance in the context of a vigorous approach to mission.

> **"**Baptism is the sign that marks the beginning of the Christian life within the community of the Church, and is to be administered to a person only once ...
>
> "Baptism incorporates a person into the local community of the Church ...
>
> "Baptism incorporates a person into the universal community of the Church.**"** (Report of the Panel on Doctrine, 2003)

Said or sung

This is not the only place for music. Throughout the service, hymns remind us of the meaning of baptism, bring back our own baptism, and connect us with the baptised through the ages. In choosing hymns, avoid the simple and the sentimental, selecting robust and memorable statements of the new life into which people are entering.

17

8 **Promise**

The minister says to the parents/godparents/sponsors:

This child belongs to God in Christ.
From this day *she* will be at home
in the Christian community,
and there will always be a place for *her*.
Tell *her* of *her* baptism,
and **unfold to *her* the treasure
she has been given today,**
so that *she* may know *she* is baptised,
and, as *she* grows,
make *her* own response in faith and love,
and come in due time
to share in the communion
of the body and blood of Christ.

Do you promise,
depending on the grace of God,
to teach this child
the truths and duties of the Christian faith;
and by prayer and example
to bring *her* up in the life
and worship of the Church?

I do.

[*In the case of an adult not proceeding to Confirmation, the minister says:*
N ..., your baptism makes you a member in Christ, and brings you into the
family of God. Now your home is in the Christian community, and you will
always have a place in it. Do you promise, depending on the grace of God,
to serve the Lord and to continue in the fellowship of the Church all the days
of your life? *To this the candidate answers:* **I do.**]

Do you promise ...?

Following the baptism of a child, the parents promise to teach their child about the Christian faith; they also promise 'by prayer and example to bring (the child) up in the life and worship of the Church'. Here, therefore, is a process rather than a one-off event. The baptism itself is not a Christian upbringing any more than school enrolment is education; there must also be a continuing nurture.

The Church of Scotland, in the first place, welcomes for baptism children whose parents, one or both, are communicant members of the Church, or are baptised and wish to become communicant members, or are baptised adherents. It also welcomes for baptism children whose parents are not known or from whom they are now separated, and who are under Christian care and guardianship. An approach regarding baptism from parents who do not fall into these categories could be an opportunity for a discussion about their own relationship to the Church.

However, given today's society where familial child-care, parent–child relationships and patterns of believing and belonging are widely varied, an Act approved by the General Assembly of 2003 acknowledged that the link between the child and the Church might be through close family members other than the parents. Those most prominent in presenting the child and making the promises on his/her behalf may be a grandparent or other close relative or friend, much as in other traditions in other times godparents made the vows in place of the parents.

Unfold to her the treasure she has been given ...

Parents and congregations should think of imaginative ways of 'telling someone of their baptism' in the years to come. In the family, the anniversary of a child's baptism may be observed to keep its 'memory' alive, confirming the child's identity just as does a birthday; in the Church, an annual or occasional invitation might be extended to all baptised children and their parents, perhaps at a special season. An ancient tradition was for a candle to be lit from the Paschal candle and given to the child. Some Reformed churches today have recovered this practice, presenting the lighted candle at the end of the service, which is then carried out by the family, to be lit, perhaps, on each anniversary of the baptism. This is equally appropriate for adult candidates. The candle may also be used in any act of reaffirmation of baptism during a person's life.

---

9 **Confirmation**

The minister says:

N ... ,
your baptism makes you a member of Christ,
and brings you into the family of God.
Now your home is in the Christian community,
and you will always have a place in it.

Believing in one God,
Father, Son, and Holy Spirit,
and confessing Jesus Christ
as your Saviour and Lord,
do you promise to join regularly
with your fellow Christians
in worship on the Lord's day?
                    I do.

Do you promise
to be faithful in reading the Bible,
and in prayer?
                    I do.

Do you promise
to give a fitting proportion
of your time, talents and money
for the Church's work in the world?
                    I do.

Do you promise,
depending on the grace of God,
to profess publicly your loyalty to Jesus Christ,
to serve him in your daily work,
and to walk his ways all the days of your life?
                    I do.

[Alternative questions may be found in Appendix A]

The meaning of Confirmation

In the early days of the Church, the whole ceremony of Christian initiation took place on the one occasion, but later the laying on of hands by the bishop which sealed the relationship of the new Christian to the Church became separated – but still part of the baptism. In time, the Church gave additional meaning to Confirmation, and as well as being a Spirit-led completing of a person's baptism it marked the entry into full participation in the councils of the Church. In our own tradition, central to the 'new status' of the baptised was their Admission to the Lord's Supper (one of the titles used in *Common Order* for this rite), signifying that they had now come to a mature understanding of the faith that had its fullest celebration at the Lord's Table. Normally in our tradition this takes place not before someone's mid- to late teens (although at the time of the Reformation this would happen between the ages of 7 and 11), usually preceded by preparation classes.

Today there is wide discussion of the relationship of baptism to 'confirmation'. It is now usually acknowledged that baptism is itself 'complete' as the entry into membership of the Church, and in the Church of Scotland baptised children are welcomed to Communion when parents desire and the kirk session permits this, a practice shared by many denominations today. In due course, these children would be confirmed in the regular way. To avoid the suggestion that confirmation is a 'final' step and that no more growth is expected thereafter, some prefer to see this event as, rather, the 'first public affirmation' of baptism.

In confirmation, a baptised person is given a responsible role in the local Church as well as in the mission of the Church in the world. The vows made are of such importance that they are approved by the General Assembly and are periodically revised to take full account of the ever-evolving shape of the Church's life and mission. New Vows and a Charge to the Congregation were agreed by the General Assembly as recently as 1996, after the publication of *Common Order*; these are set out in Appendix A and may be substituted for those printed here.

It is customary, but not necessary, for candidates for baptism to be dressed appropriately for the occasion. In the ancient Church, there was a tradition of wearing white (hence 'Whit' Sunday for Pentecost, a special day for baptisms). People have long felt in our tradition that when presenting children for baptism white garments are appropriate. Some Churches in the Reformed tradition are returning to a version of this early practice for adults also, with the garments being made for the occasion by themselves or by friends, perhaps incorporating Christian symbols upon the material.

The new member kneels, and the minister lays hands on her *head and says:*

Defend, O Lord, your servant *N* ...,
with your heavenly grace,
that *she* may continue yours for ever,
and daily increase in your Holy Spirit
until *she* comes into your everlasting kingdom.

The new member stands.
The minister says:

In the name of the Lord Jesus Christ,
the King and Head of the Church,
and by the authority of this kirk session,
I welcome and receive you
within the fellowship of the Lord's Table,
and admit you
to the full privileges of the children of God
and to the responsibilities of membership
within this congregation
of the one holy catholic and apostolic Church.
May your sharing in our life together
bring blessing to you and to us all.

The peace of the Lord Jesus be always with you.
And also with you.

The minister and kirk session greet her *and offer the right hand of fellowship. The district elder may give* her *a Bible.*

Baptism and Holy Communion

The laying on of hands is an ancient tradition symbolising the strengthening power of the Holy Spirit. It is in the strength of the Holy Spirit that the baptised/confirmed person continues life in Christ, and part of this continuing life is participation in the sacrament of Holy Communion. In sacraments, the worshipping community offers up patterns of words, symbols and actions through which it prays that the Lord of the Church may strengthen, challenge and comfort his people. Baptism is the sacrament of entrance to membership of the Church and occurs once in a Christian's life; Holy Communion, on the other hand, offers Church and individual continual nourishment which may be drawn upon repeatedly. As well as being the continuing bond between a person and Christ, it binds together the people of the Church, local, world-wide, and ages-long.

66 In 1 Corinthians 10 ... Paul uses the imagery of baptism in order to explain the exodus experience of the people of Israel under Moses. Thus, the people of Israel are said to have been baptised in their escape from Egypt, where they are led by the pillars of cloud and fire (Exodus 13:21–2) and pass through the Red Sea (Exodus 14:21–2). This interpretation is set within an attempt to understand the Lord's Supper in terms of the relationship, and the contrast, between God's provision in the Old Testament and the provision made through Christ (1 Corinthians 10:1–4, 16–17). 99 (Report of the Panel on Doctrine, 2003)

The minister and kirk session greet ...

In the case of adults, to express this welcome, some congregations make room here for the greeting/embracing of the newly baptised person(s) by other members of the congregation. In the case of babies or children, they may be presented to or led round the congregation. Some involve children from the church in this welcome, with a child giving flowers to the mother of the baby.

---

10   **Commitment of Congregation**

You who are gathered here
represent the whole Church,
the Church catholic.
Word and Sacrament bring you
the joy of Christ's presence in your midst.
They also bring you responsibilities
as Christ's people in this place.
Do you welcome *N* ... ;
and **do you renew your commitment**,
with God's help,
to live before all God's children
in a kindly and Christian way,
and to share with them
the knowledge and love of Christ?

The congregation says:

We do.

The minister and congregation say together:

***We will nurture one another in faith,
uphold one another in prayer,
encourage one another in service.***

[An alternative version may be found as part of Appendix A]

11   **Prayers**

God of love, we rejoice again
to receive your grace in Word and Sacrament.
We have heard your call
and are made new by your Spirit.

Do you renew your commitment ...?

One of the emphases emerging ecumenically is that the 'rite', the event, of baptism, for its fullest expression requires not only an adequate period of preparation but also a 'receiving body' which both gives nurture to and receives new life from the newly baptised. More attention needs to be given to the continuing formation of baptised persons within the body of Christ. Too often, they may feel that they have reached the end of a process rather than embarking on a new and active stage. The congregation may appear not to value them or expect much from them, except perhaps in sharing out some of the day-to-day responsibilities involved in running a church. By contrast, a lively congregation will encourage those who are now part of its life as well as reap the benefit of their talents and gifts.

The General Assembly of 1996 (see Appendix A) decided not just to sharpen the vows taken by those being confirmed but also to emphasise that the congregation was not an onlooker but an active participant. To give a 'charge' is to lay a solemn and serious responsibility upon someone. To 'love, encourage and support' is not simply to express vague feelings of good will but also to ensure that the life and structures of the local church actively enfold the newly baptised or confirmed member.

The local church needs continually to examine its life to ensure:

- that it truly seeks to encounter and listen to Christ in its midst – in preaching, teaching, study and prayer, as well as through service in his name;
- that the style of its life together and of its individual members speaks of Christ to the world, challenging injustice, caring even when costly, serving even when there is no return, declaring the gospel in ever new ways;
- that it no longer 'lives on the surface', unaware of what is really going on in the lives of its members and in the wider community;
- that it is an open community in which people from all different backgrounds will feel truly at home;
- that it continually explores what it means to be a 'loving community in Christ', 'nurturing, upholding and encouraging'.

❝We must face the truth that, for large sections of the Scottish population, the celebration of baptism has ceased to have the meaning and significance that it had for previous generations. In one sense, this is to state the obvious. However, the honest recognition of this truth within the Church of Scotland may yet lead towards the renewal of our understanding of baptism and the recovery of elements within that tradition which have been neglected or overlooked. ❞ (Report of the Panel on Doctrine, 2003)

Either

> Guide and guard *N* ... all *her* days.
> May your love hold *her*,
> your truth guide *her*,
> your joy delight *her.*
> Bless *her* parents,
> that *she* may grow up
> in a secure and happy home.
> Give to *her* family
> wisdom and courage,
> laughter and peace,
> and the love that endures all things.

or

Guide and guard *N* ... all *her* days.
May your love hold *her*,
your truth guide *her*,
your joy delight *her.*
Since you have called *her*,
and you keep faith and will do it,
make *her* holy through and through,
free of any fault,
when our Lord Jesus Christ comes
with all those who are his own.

God of grace,
in whose Church there is one Lord,
one Faith, **one Baptism**,
help us to acknowledge
that Jesus Christ is Lord,
to profess with our whole lives
the one true faith,
and to live in love and unity
with all who are baptised in his name,
through Jesus Christ our Lord,
who lives and reigns,
and is worshipped and glorified,
with you, Father, and the Holy Spirit,
one God for ever. **Amen.**

One Baptism

Sometimes a new and joyous step in faith in the life of someone already baptised – perhaps as a child – seems to demand a public celebration. The only ceremony big enough to express this has often been thought to be baptism, with its full ordered solemnity, strength of symbol, and, in the case of an adult, opportunity for declaring new commitment. But can a person be baptised again? In support of this, it may be argued that as an infant one was not able to decide for oneself but now things are different. It may also be argued that one's later confirmation was seen at the time more as a 'rite of passage' than as a step in faith.

A second baptism is understood in our Reformed tradition as impossible, not because, as is sometimes assumed, our belief about baptism is too weak but because it is so strong. Baptism is seen as an initiative taken by God himself. Prior to any decision of ours is the call and claim of God. Certainly, other circumstances may have influenced the desire of our parents to seek baptism – and the Holy Spirit in many different circumstances acts upon and turns to good purpose partial and faltering human actions – but the firm belief of the Church is that baptism does not seal and celebrate the individual's decision to come to faith but rather seals and celebrates the promises of God. We cannot add to Christ's finished work.

Once received into the body of Christ, how can we be 're-received'? The Christ whose body we become, into whose death and resurrection we are bound, died only once and was raised once. Only once can we be incorporated. Once welcomed into the family of Christ, we remain members (even if poor members), bearing the family name, enjoying the family meal.

But behind the impulse to seek a second baptism lies, nevertheless, a true understanding of the nature of baptism, namely that it is inseparably linked with faith. Faith grows continually towards Christ. It is therefore part of the event of baptism that faith is expressed – by parent or by adult believer. This, however, is not a faith achieved, for which baptism is the 'reward', but a journey of faith begun. This is likely to be a journey of many stages. To say: 'This is it' at any point (and to wish to mark it by a second 'real' baptism) is to leave unanswered the question: 'What will I do at the next stage?' Martin Luther remarked: 'Were I to be baptised on my own faith, I might tomorrow find myself unbaptised if faith failed me, or I became worried that I might not yesterday have had the faith rightly'.

Our Father ...

In addition, the following may be used:

Gracious God,
touch us all again this day
with the grace of our baptism.
Give us **new lives for old**,
new spirits, new faith, new commitment,
in place of all that has grown tired and stale
and dead in our lives.
So may we rise and go from here,
to whatever awaits us, in joy and trust.

Eternal God,
we rejoice in the communion of all the saints,
and remember with thanksgiving
those who have already passed through
the waters of death into life eternal.
May we follow them,
faithfully and expectantly,
in the strength of our baptism
in Christ Jesus our Lord,
who lives and reigns,
and is worshipped and glorified
with you, Father, and the Holy Spirit,
one God for ever.   **Amen.**

12   *The rest of the service, which may include **Holy Communion**,
    follows.*

New lives for old

The celebration of baptism encourages all who have been baptised to draw on God for our daily renewal. There is a tradition going back at least to Martin Luther of reminding ourselves daily that we have been baptised – into privileges and responsibilities. In worship, each time we confess our sins and embrace the cleansing of forgiveness, we 'retrace our steps' to the new path upon which we set out under the sign of the cleansing water of baptism. Every time we declare our faith in the Creed, we are echoing the words of the faith declared at our baptism. Each time we take the bread and the wine, we are affirming our place in the 'new covenant' to which our baptism was the entry.

It is surely right, however, to wish to mark in a significant way a new stage of growth in faith and in an event which recalls and reflects one's baptism. In some traditions the rite for the eve of Easter includes the sprinkling of the congregation with water to recall their baptism. Some Churches in the Reformed tradition have devised special services of Renewal of Baptism for individuals who have come to a new stage of faith, or for use on a significant congregational anniversary. Such a rite might take place on Easter Day or at Pentecost, traditional times for baptism in the earlier Church. The 'Covenant Service' on p. 343 of *Common Order* (1996) is intended for such a purpose and has been found to be both moving and meaningful.

Holy Communion

Baptism, the rite of entry into the life of Christ and the church, unites us with all who have been likewise baptised; and there is here an intimate connection with the sacrament of Holy Communion. Invited to anticipate the heavenly banquet, we enact our common belonging in the power of the Holy Spirit as we receive bread and wine in remembrance that Christ lived and died for us. While the practice of the Church of Scotland has often been to keep the two sacraments apart, bringing them together powerfully underscores our dependence on Christ. Alone we may wander far, even having been baptised; with Christ feeding our hunger and quenching our thirst, we keep close to the source of life in its fullness.

A Pastoral Issue: Baptism or 'Blessing'?

The story of Jesus rebuking the disciples and saying: 'Let the children come to me' (Luke 18:16–17) used to be one of the first passages read in services of baptism. In the present service, it is one of several options which can be added after the prescribed passages are read. There is a reason for this.

For the last few centuries in the Church of Scotland, there has been a strong emphasis on infant baptism, and most recently this has been accepted as the norm. However, the baptism report at the General Assembly of 2003, having revisited the Church's own earlier documents, having reviewed discussions in the world Church and the situation facing us in our own nation in the present day, and having embarked upon a renewed study of the gospels, suggested that adult and infant baptism, both part of our tradition, should more evidently be given equal place.

Another proposal was accepted by the Assembly. The situation in Scotland today was described as one of 'primary mission'; in 1961, some 50 per cent of infants were baptised in the Church of Scotland, but by 2001, the number had shrunk to around 20 per cent. In addition, many parents who approached the Church seeking baptism for their children today did not realise the continuing implications of the baptism of their child, yet they wanted to relate the child publicly to God, and sought an event which would bring the child within the sphere of God's influence. Further, some parents today preferred to allow their children to make their own mature decision about baptism yet wished to have the child acknowledged as part of the Church family.

Thus it was agreed to prepare orders for thanksgiving and blessing at the birth or adoption of a child which could be used for both the above circumstances. Care would be taken so that in content or practice it would not be confused with baptism. These are now published under the title, *A Welcome to a Child* (Saint Andrew Press).

> **"A service of Blessing finds a close precedent in the ministry of Jesus himself. It seems clear from the evidence of the New Testament that, within the circle of the disciples of Jesus, the practice of baptism was complemented by the practice of blessing, such that, in the Gospel incidents recorded, when children were brought to Jesus he blessed them."** (Report of the Panel on Doctrine, 2003)

APPENDIX A

Vows and Charge to the Congregation

Authorised by the General Assembly of 1996

(These may replace the sections on the vows of baptismal candidates and the commitment of the congregation in the Adult Baptism and Confirmation services in *Common Order.*)

We ask you now to pledge yourself to a life of Christian discipleship.

Do you promise to follow Jesus Christ in your daily life?

**With God's help
I will seek to follow Christ,
and in listening for God's Word,
in the breaking of bread, and prayer,
to grow ever closer to him as the years pass.**

Do you promise to be a faithful member of the Christian community?

**With God's help
I will share in the worship and service of the Church,
and in this I will give generously
of what I am and what I have.**

Do you promise to take your part in God's mission to the world?

**With God's help
I will witness to Christ
wherever I find myself
and putting my trust and hope in him
I will seek justice and peace
and the renewing of all life
according to God's promise.**

[*or the responses may be put in the form of questions by the minister
– for example, 'Do you promise, with God's help …?', the candidate
answering: 'With God's help I will'.*]

31

The minister then gives a charge to the congregation in such words as:

I charge you,
the people of this congregation,
to love, encourage and support
these our brothers and sisters in faith,
that *they* may continue to grow
in the grace of the Lord Jesus Christ
and the knowledge and love of God.

The congregation responds:

**With God's help
we will live out our baptism
as a loving community in Christ:
nurturing one another in faith,
upholding one another in prayer,
and encouraging one another in service.**

APPENDIX B

The Doctrine of Baptism

from Report of Panel on Doctrine to General Assembly 2003

Baptism signifies the action and love of God in Christ, through the Holy Spirit, and is a seal upon the gift of grace and the response of faith.

Baptism is to be administered in the name of the Father and of the Son and of the Holy Spirit, with water, by sprinkling, pouring, or immersion.

The meaning of baptism is rooted in the life, death and resurrection of Jesus Christ.

The call to baptise is rooted in the command of the Gospel of Jesus Christ.

The promise of baptism is rooted in the giving of the Holy Spirit on the day of Pentecost.

Baptism is the sign that marks the beginning of the Christian life within the community of the Church, and is to be administered to a person only once.

Baptism incorporates a person into the local community of the Church.

Baptism incorporates a person into the universal community of the Church.

The primary image of baptism in the New Testament is that of a person being baptised upon personal profession of faith.

The primary image of the New Testament is complemented by the image of the baptism of the household upon corporate profession of faith.